QUEENSLAND
VACATION GUIDE
2023

The Essential and Ultimate Guide to Queensland's Hotels, Cuisines, Shopping Tips, Insider's Tips, Top Attractions, History, and Culture

ALFRED FLORES

TABLE OF CONTENTS

INTRODUCTION

Welcome to the vivacious and enchanting state of Queensland, where cosmopolitan cities, lush rainforests, and sun-kissed beaches combine together to make for an amazing trip. Queensland, located in Australia's northeast, entices visitors with its varied landscapes, rich cultural history, and wealth of exhilarating adventures. The Queensland Vacation Guide 2023 is your ultimate and indispensable travel guide for exploring the delights of this unique location, whether you are an experienced traveler or setting off on your first Australian adventure.

We welcome you to embark on a journey of discovery as we reveal the hidden treasures and must-see sights that characterize Queensland within the pages of this thorough guidebook. We spare no effort in our mission to highlight the finest of

Queensland, from the busy cityscapes of Brisbane and the renowned Gold Coast to the pristine coasts of the Whitsundays and the age-old wonders of the Daintree Rainforest.

This guidebook goes beyond the obvious and provides a deeper grasp of Queensland's history and culture to ensure an enriching and immersive trip. Discover the state's deep Indigenous heritage, from the ancient customs of the Aboriginal peoples to the thriving modern art scene that honors their lasting legacy. Discover how Queensland's colonial past affected the state by immersing yourself in the enthralling tales told about it.

Without indulging in the mouth watering local cuisine, a trip isn't complete, and Queensland delights with its wide variety of cuisines. Whether you're in the mood for freshly caught seafood, mouthwatering tropical fruits, or fusion cuisine that combines worldwide influences, our guide will point you in the direction of the best restaurants and undiscovered culinary gems.

Beyond the alluring views and tastes, our book also provides insightful expert advice and shopping suggestions to improve your experience in Queensland. Find the greatest places for retail therapy, whether you're looking for trendy boutiques, neighborhood markets, or distinctive artisanal goods. Learn how to use Queensland's transportation systems, so you may effortlessly travel the state's wide territory and get to even the most remote locations.

It's important to select the ideal lodging if you want to fully experience Queensland. Each hotel, resort, and lodge listed in our directory has been hand-picked for its great quality, welcoming atmosphere, and close access to the state's most popular tourist destinations. We have hand-selected the top options to suit every style and budget, whether you're looking for an opulent seaside retreat, a jungle hideaway, or a buzzing downtown hotel.

More than just a travel companion, The Queensland Vacation Guide 2023 is an invitation to set off on a magnificent voyage of discovery, exploration, and adventure. Pack your luggage, be open to the delights that lie ahead, and let us be your dependable guide as you make lifelong memories amid Queensland's beautiful beauty.

Get ready for a remarkable adventure; the voyage has just begun.

CHAPTER ONE:
Discovering Queensland

Geographical Overview

Queensland, a large and diversified state that has an area of around 1.85 million square kilometers (715,300 square miles), is located in the northeastern region of Australia. It extends from the Pacific Ocean's glistening coastlines in the east to the Great Dividing Range's rough terrain in the west. The state is a hub for discovering the wonders of the Australian Continent because it shares borders with New South Wales, the Northern Territory, and South Australia.

The landscapes of Queensland are remarkably diverse, ranging from lovely sandy beaches and tropical islands to deep rainforests, vast outback areas, and energetic urban centers. Along

Queensland's coastline, the Great Barrier Reef, a UNESCO World Heritage site, offers unrivaled opportunities for snorkeling, diving, and exploring the largest coral reef system in the world.

Climate and Weather

Queensland has a primarily subtropical climate with distinct wet and dry seasons, mild temperatures, and lots of sunshine. The state has moderate winters and hot, muggy summers, though there are regional differences.

The climate is generally pleasant year-round in coastal regions, including the well-known tourist sites of the Gold Coast and Sunshine Coast, with average temperatures ranging from 20°C to 30°C (68°F to 86°F) in the summer and 10°C to 22°C (50°F to 72°F) in the winter. The climate is more tropical in the tropical north, which includes places like Cairns and the Daintree Rainforest, with higher temperatures and a rainy season from November to April that brings cool rain showers.

History and Culture

Queensland has a long, rich Indigenous history that dates back thousands of years. The Turrbal, Yuggera, Jagera, and other Aboriginal peoples have lived in this area for tens of thousands of years, cultivating a strong bond with the land and passing down their cultural traditions to future generations.

Although early 17th-century European exploration of the area began, Queensland didn't begin to take shape as a distinct colony until British settlers arrived in the 19th century. A substantial amount of expansion and migration occurred in the state as a result of the discovery of gold and the development of agricultural businesses. Following its official declaration as a separate colony in 1859, Queensland later changed its status to a state within the newly formed Commonwealth of Australia in 1901.

Today, a wide range of influences are woven into Queensland's cultural fabric. It welcomes the pluralism that generations of immigrants from throughout the world have brought, honors its Indigenous past, and supports a thriving modern arts scene. Through museums, art galleries, performances, and encounters with the local communities, visitors to Queensland can experience and participate in this rich cultural diversity.

Festivals and Events

Queensland has a reputation for hosting exciting festivals and events that highlight the state's cultural diversity, artistic brilliance, and love of celebration.

Visitors and locals alike may immerse themselves in a schedule chock-full of thrilling events that cater to a variety of interests throughout the year.

A major event in Queensland's cultural calendar is the Brisbane Festival, which takes place every September. The event culminates in the spectacular Riverfire fireworks display over the Brisbane River and offers a fascinating program of music, dance, theater, and visual arts.

The Woodford Folk Festival is a well-liked occasion that draws performers and guests from all over the world. It lasts for six days in late December to early January. The festival honors music, the arts, cultural seminars, and group spirit while taking place in the lovely hamlet of Woodford.

For sports enthusiasts, the State of Origin Rugby League series between Queensland and New South

Wales is a fiercely contested event that captivates the entire state. The electrifying atmosphere in the stadiums and the passionate support of the teams make it a truly memorable experience for sports fans.

Other notable festivals and events include the Gold Coast 600, an exciting motorsport event that draws racing enthusiasts from all over the world, the Noosa Food and Wine Festival, where gastronomic delights take center stage, and the Cairns Indigenous Art Fair, which highlights the talents of Aboriginal and Torres Strait Islander artists.

Visitors have a rare chance to experience Queensland's colorful culture firsthand, interact with the locals, and forge lifelong memories at these festivals and events.

The Queensland Vacation Guide 2023 has a wealth of knowledge about the geography, climate, history, and cultural attractions of the state. We cordially encourage you to embrace Queensland's spirit and take part in the celebrations that highlight the state's breathtaking natural beauty, rich cultural history, and welcoming people. Get ready to be mesmerized by the stunning scenery, enthralled by the historical tales, and motivated by the vivacious tapestry of cultures that make Queensland such an extraordinary travel destination.

CHAPTER TWO:
Planning Your Trip to Queensland

Best Time to Travel

To get the most of your trip, it is essential to visit Queensland during the proper time of year. Although the state has a pleasant environment all year round, distinct locations could experience varied weather patterns and seasonal highlights.

From December to February, during the Australian summer, is Queensland's busiest travel period. Warm temperatures throughout this time make it ideal for water sports and beach activities. However, congested areas and more expensive lodging are possible in well-known locations. If you want to go during this period, it's best to make reservations in advance.

The shoulder seasons of spring (September to November) and autumn (March to May) are great options if you want milder temperatures and fewer tourists. These times of year bring beautiful weather, burgeoning flowers, and the chance to take part in festivals and events.

Queensland's winter, which lasts from June to August, is often moderate, especially near the shore. The north's tropical areas are ideal for exploration now that the weather is still comfortably warm. Humpback whales migrate along the coast of Queensland during the winter, making it the ideal time to go whale watching.

Visa and Travel Requirements

Understanding the visa and travel requirements for entering Australia is crucial before beginning your Queensland vacation. The majority of travelers will need to apply for an Australian visa; the kind you need depends on your country and the reason for your trip.

Most tourists can apply for an Electronic Travel Authority (ETA) or an eVisitor visa online for short-term travel. The Australian Department of Home Affairs website or travel agencies make it simple to apply for these visas, which are valid for stays of up to three months. For the most recent information on visa requirements specific to your country of residency, it is suggested to visit the official Australian government website.

Additionally, visitors visiting Queensland should make sure their passports are current and have at least six months remaining on them after their anticipated departure date. It's also crucial to have travel insurance that pays for unexpected events and medical costs.

How to Get There

With numerous large airports offering both domestic and international flights, Queensland is conveniently accessible by air. Brisbane Airport, which provides links to numerous places across the world, serves as the main international gateway. Other significant airports are located in the north at Cairns Airport, the south at Gold Coast Airport, and the center at Townsville Airport.

Major locations including Los Angeles, Singapore, Dubai, and Hong Kong all have direct flights that land at Brisbane Airport for international passengers. From major Australian cities including Sydney, Melbourne, and Perth, a variety of airlines offer flights to Queensland's airports for domestic travelers to pick from.

When you get to Queensland, you can travel in a variety of ways to see the whole state. For getting between major cities and regions, there are domestic flights, train services, and coach services accessible. In order to independently explore Queensland, many people choose to rent a car, which gives them the opportunity to travel to far-flung locations and enjoy scenic drives.

The Pacific Coast Highway offers breathtaking views and the chance to explore quaint coastal communities, and it connects Queensland's coastal regions well by road. As an alternative, you can use the effective public transportation networks found in major cities and popular tourist destinations, such as trains, buses, and ferries.

Getting Around

To make the most of your visit and to assist you get around the state, Queensland provides a range of transportation alternatives.

1. Domestic Flights: Queensland has a number of domestic airports that connect its major metropolitan areas with its regional hubs. There are frequent flights between destinations thanks to airlines like Qantas, Virgin Australia, and Jetstar. This is especially helpful for traveling rapidly over vast distances or getting to farther-flung locations.

2. Trains: Queensland Rail runs a network of trains that connects key cities and offers beautiful rides. From Brisbane to Cairns, passengers can take the well-liked Spirit of Queensland train, which features plush seats, overnight beds, and panoramic windows to take in the stunning scenery.

3. Bus and coach services are provided for both local and long-distance travel. It is a cost-effective solution for visiting Queensland because organizations like Greyhound and Premier Motor Service provide easy itineraries and frequent departures. Within cities and towns, public buses run, offering dependable transportation for short distances.

4. Car Rental: Renting a car provides you the flexibility to explore Queensland at your own speed and reach farther-flung destinations. In airports and cities all around the state, there are offices of significant vehicle rental businesses. Understand the local driving laws, the state of the roads, and any additional requirements, such as those for international driving licenses.

5. Ferries and Cruises: Ferry and cruise services provide convenient access to Queensland's coastline

and islands. You may travel by ferry from the mainland to places like the Whitsundays, Fraser Island, and the Great Barrier Reef. A unique way to experience Queensland's natural splendor is on a river cruise along the Daintree or Brisbane rivers.

Accommodation Options

Queensland provides a wide selection of lodging choices to fit every need, preference, and way of traveling.

1. Hotels and Resorts: Queensland's major cities and tourist attractions provide a wide array of lodging options, ranging from five-star luxury hotels to boutique resorts. These places provide welcoming facilities, first-rate service, and practical locations—often with easy access to gorgeous beaches or other natural attractions.

2. Apartments and Holiday Homes: Renting apartments or vacation houses is a great choice for families, groups, or individuals looking for a more independent setting. Self-contained lodging offers the convenience of kitchenettes, many bedrooms, and roomy living spaces. Cities, coastal communities, and rural locations all contain them.

3. Backpacker Hostels: Queensland is a well-liked vacation spot for visitors on a tight budget, and there are lots of hostels that cater to this market. These hostels provide individual rooms or shared dormitory-style accommodations at reasonable prices. They frequently have kitchens, social rooms, and planned activities, making it easy to meet other tourists.

4. Camping and Caravan Parks: Queensland offers a variety of camping and caravan sites for people looking to get closer to nature. Beautiful campsites

with few amenities are available in national parks, coastal areas, and rural areas. For campers and RV travelers, caravan parks offer facilities such powered sites, amenity blocks, and common spaces.

Travel Insurance

When visiting Queensland or any other foreign location, getting travel insurance is highly advised. Travel insurance offers protection against unforeseen circumstances including trip cancellations, medical emergencies, misplaced luggage, or travel delays.

Make sure the travel insurance you choose includes medical costs, evacuation in case of emergency, trip cancellation or interruption, personal liability, and loss or theft of property. Choose a plan that meets your needs by carefully reading the policy's specifics, including any exclusions or limitations.

To provide coverage for any unanticipated events that may occur before or during your stay to Queensland, it is important to buy travel insurance as soon as you make your reservation. Choose an insurance provider after doing some research on them, comparing their services, and looking at their customer testimonials.

Having travel insurance provides peace of mind, knowing that you have financial protection in case of unforeseen circumstances when traveling gives you peace of mind. Always keep your insurance information and emergency contact information with you.

In conclusion, Queensland has a variety of transportation choices, enabling you to effortlessly explore the state. These include aircraft, trains, buses, vehicle rentals, and ferry services. To suit various tastes and budgets, lodging options range from hotels and resorts to apartments, hostels, and camping areas. Make getting travel insurance a top priority to protect yourself from unforeseen circumstances and guarantee a stress-free trip.

Think about the ideal time to visit Queensland based on your tastes and the experiences you want to have as you prepare for your vacation there. Make sure you are aware of the visa requirements and that you have all the required paperwork. Plan your travel, lodging, and insurance in advance to get the greatest discounts. Research and book your flights and accommodations beforehand. By being well-prepared, you may travel to Queensland with confidence and be ready to fully immerse yourself in its charms.

CHAPTER THREE:
Exploring Queensland's Regions

The many regions of Queensland provide a wide range of extraordinary experiences and magnificent scenery. We'll focus on Brisbane and Surrounds, Gold Coast, Sunshine Coast, and Tropical North Queensland as our four main areas.

Brisbane and Surroundings

Brisbane, the capital of Queensland, is a thriving center for arts, entertainment, and delectable cuisine. Visit the Queensland Museum and Gallery of Modern Art, relax in the lush gardens, and stroll along the picturesque Brisbane River when you explore the South Bank neighborhood. Enjoy top-notch dining establishments in Fortitude Valley's bustling streets or try regional fare at its lively markets.

Explore the areas surrounding Brisbane to see their natural beauty. Visit one of the picturesque Moreton Bay Islands for the day to take advantage of the pristine beaches, sandboarding, kayaking, and snorkeling opportunities. These islands include North Stradbroke Island and Moreton Island. As an alternative, visit the quaint rural communities of the Scenic Rim, which are renowned for their breathtaking national parks, hiking trails, and farm excursions.

Gold Coast

The Gold Coast offers a thrilling fusion of leisure and adventure and is renowned for its golden sand beaches, top-notch theme parks, and dynamic nightlife. Discover the city's center, Surfers Paradise, where you can dine by the ocean, browse at upscale stores, or go surfing. Visit renowned sites including Sea World and Warner Bros. You can find exhilarating rides and entertainment at Movie World or Dreamworld.

Located in the hinterland of the Gold Coast, Australia's Gondwana Rainforests are on the UNESCO World Heritage List. Discover the lush rainforests, tumbling waterfalls, and spectacular vistas of Lamington National Park or Springbrook National Park. A robust arts and culture scene, including galleries, exhibits, and live performances, is also available on the Gold Coast.

Sunshine Coast

With its gorgeous beaches, clean oceans, and laid-back coastal way of life, the Sunshine Coast is a beach lover's paradise. A must-see location, Noosa Heads is recognized for its magnificent national park, fashionable Hastings Street dotted with shops and eateries, and the lovely Noosa Main Beach. At the nearby Noosa Everglades, where you can kayak through tranquil canals and see unusual species, get close to nature.

Explore the thriving coastal communities of Mooloolaba, Maroochydore, and Caloundra further south; each has its own allure and attractions. The gorgeous hinterland towns of Montville and Maleny, where you can peruse art galleries, savor regional fare, and take in stunning vistas of the Glass House Mountains, make up the Sunshine Coast Hinterland, a haven for nature lovers.

Tropical North Queensland

Tropical North Queensland is home to amazing natural beauties and a diverse culture. As the entryway to the Great Barrier Reef, Cairns provides options for sailing, scuba diving, and snorkeling excursions. Visit Kuranda, a charming village in a rainforest, by taking a scenic train trip, or experience breathtaking panoramic views by riding the Skyrail Rainforest Cableway above the treetops.

Visit the Daintree Rainforest, the oldest tropical rainforest still in existence, for a really authentic rainforest experience. Go on guided walks, see unusual species, and discover the area's rich Indigenous history. Port Douglas, a charming coastal community nearby, provides easy access to the beautiful Mossman Gorge as well as a laid-back environment and clean beaches.

Don't pass up the chance to discover the verdant farmlands, waterfalls, and volcanic lakes of the Atherton Tablelands. Take advantage of the lively markets to sample regional fare, cool down in freshwater swimming holes, and admire the breathtaking Curtain Fig Tree and Millaa Mill Waterfalls.

Whitsunday Islands

The Whitsunday Islands, which are in the center of the Great Barrier Reef, are a genuine tropical haven. These 74 magnificent islands provide beautiful beaches, blue oceans, and an abundance of marine life. Sailing across the Whitsundays is a well-liked method of discovering this magnificent archipelago. It enables you to stop at famous locations like Hill Inlet, where the swirling patterns of sand and water create a captivating spectacle, and Whitehaven Beach, noted for its pristine white silica sand. It is essential to snorkel or dive in the coral gardens of the Great Barrier Reef to get a close-up look at the thriving marine ecology.

Great Barrier Reef

A UNESCO World Heritage site and one of nature's most amazing wonders, the Great Barrier Reef stretches for more than 2,300 kilometers (1,430 miles) along Queensland's coast. Marine life is abundant in this thriving coral habitat, including colorful fish, turtles, and majestic manta rays. Explore the reef on snorkeling or scuba diving tours to see the array of coral formations and fascinating marine life that it is home to. The Great Barrier Reef is accessible from a number of coastal cities, including Cairns and Port Douglas, which also provide a variety of reef excursions, cruises, and educational opportunities to help you understand this natural wonder.

Cairns and Far North Queensland

Far North Queensland's bustling metropolis of Cairns serves as a starting point for exploring the area's tropical attractions. From here, you may go out on jungle excursions to explore the historic Daintree jungle and its distinctive environment. To see crocodiles, birds, and other wildlife, go on a river tour along the Daintree River. The Cairns area is well-known for its exhilarating activities, including skydiving, bungee jumping, and white-water rafting, for thrill-seekers.

If you travel further north, the charming town of Port Douglas offers access to the Great Barrier Reef and the breathtaking Mossman Gorge, where you may discover the Indigenous spirituality of the area. The adjacent Atherton Tablelands provide waterfalls, beautiful scenery, and the chance to sample delectable tropical fruit.

Outback Queensland

Visit Outback Queensland if you want to experience Australia's truly untamed side. This huge area includes immense plains, wide-open deserts, and old cities that perfectly capture the nation's pioneering spirit. By traveling to locations like Longreach, where you can explore the Australian Stockman's Hall of Fame and discover the history of the cattle ranching in the area, you can experience the rich heritage of Outback Queensland. Explore the Carnarvon Gorge's red sandstone scenery and see prehistoric Aboriginal rock art.

By taking the Savannah Way, a long road trip route that runs from Cairns to Broome and passes through outlying communities, national parks, and well-known sites, you can see the grandeur of the Outback. Enjoy the amazing vistas of the Simpson Desert, the magnificent Undara Lava Tubes, and the Boodjamulla (Lawn Hill) National Park.

You may connect with the area's rich history and culture while experiencing the untamed beauty of Australia's environment in Outback Queensland, which offers an authentic and inspiring experience.

You'll come across a patchwork of natural beauty, thrilling attractions, and cultural experiences as you travel across various parts of Queensland. Each area provides chances for exploration, adventure, and leisure in addition to its own special charm. Each destination promises to foster lifelong memories and a profound connection, whether you choose to wander through the energetic streets of Brisbane, catch waves on the Gold Coast, relax in the Sunshine Coast's laid-back atmosphere, immerse yourself in the wonders of Tropical North Queensland, sail through the Whitsunday Islands, snorkel in the Great Barrier Reef, explore the rainforests of Cairns, or go on an outback adventure.

CHAPTER FOUR:
Uncovering Hidden Gems in Queensland

Queensland is renowned for its hidden treasures that provide distinctive and off-the-beaten-path experiences in addition to its well-known tourist spots. The following are some of Queensland's undiscovered hidden gems:

National Parks and Rainforests

Queensland is home to numerous national parks and tropical rainforests, which highlight the state's incredible biodiversity and scenic splendor. Discover the magnificent rainforests, cascading waterfalls, and hiking paths of Lamington National Park in the Gold Coast hinterland. Another must-see is the well-known Mossman Gorge, which is located in the Daintree Rainforest close to Cairns. Here, you may swim in pristine waters and discover the region's rich Indigenous heritage. Avoid missing Girringun National Park on the Cassowary Coast area, which is home to the magnificent Wallaman Falls, Australia's biggest single-drop waterfall.

Waterfalls and Swimming Holes

Beautiful waterfalls and natural swimming holes may be found all around Queensland, offering calming getaways. Visit Josephine Falls near Innisfail to enjoy swimming in crystal-clear pools and sliding down natural rock slides. In the beautiful rainforest of Cairns, Crystal Cascades provides a number of flowing waterfalls and tranquil swimming holes. Visit Millaa Millaa Falls, which is well-known for its stunning splendor and the opportunity to bathe beneath the cascading waters, while exploring the Atherton Tablelands. These undiscovered treasures provide chances to unwind and experience nature in a special and immersive way.

Islands and Beaches

The coastline of Queensland is dotted with various islands and quiet beaches that provide serenity and spectacular views. Off the coast of Townsville sits Magnetic Island, a hidden gem with gorgeous beaches, hiking paths, and the opportunity to see wild koalas in their native environment. Visit the lesser-known Fitzroy Island near Cairns where you can climb through lush jungle trails and explore the fringing coral reefs. Explore the Capricorn Coast to find a distant and unspoiled beach experience. Here, the picturesque Keppel Bay Islands provide pristine beaches, possibilities for snorkeling, and chances to see wildlife.

Wildlife Encounters

Unique and diverse wildlife abounds in Queensland, and there are secret spots where you can see these animals in their natural settings. As you stroll through the spectacular gorge at Carnarvon Gorge in Outback Queensland, you might see rock wallabies, platypus, and several bird species. There are possibilities to swim or dive with sea turtles, manta rays, and vibrant fish in the Southern Great Barrier Reef zone, which includes Lady Elliot Island and Heron Island. The Daintree Rainforest, located farther north, is home to a wide variety of fauna, including cassowaries, tree kangaroos, and several bird species.

Aboriginal Cultural Experiences

Explore Queensland's rich Aboriginal tradition and culture by looking for undiscovered attractions that provide genuine encounters. Join an Indigenous-led tour to discover the culture, history, and relationship to the land of the Quandamooka people in the Quandamooka region near Brisbane. Join a cultural trip with the Ngaro Aboriginal people in the Whitsunday region to learn about their customs, storytelling, and the significance of the islands. In the vicinity of Cairns, the Tjapukai Aboriginal Cultural Park presents live performances, hands-on exhibits, and instructive activities that highlight the rich customs of the regional Indigenous people.

You can discover lesser-known facets of Queensland's natural treasures, interact with locals, and forge lifelong memories by exploring these hidden jewels that are off the beaten tourist track. These undiscovered gems urge you to engage with the natural world, immerse yourself in cultural practices, and experience Queensland's beauty in its most natural and unspoiled state. Discovering quiet waterfalls, observing amazing animals, or interacting with Aboriginal people are just a few of the hidden treasures that help you gain a deeper understanding of what makes Queensland so exceptional.

CHAPTER FIVE:
Queensland's Natural Wonders

The state of Queensland is known for its incredible natural beauties, and it is home to some of the most famous and magnificent landscapes in the entire globe. Let's examine five extraordinary natural wonders in Queensland in greater detail:

Great Barrier Reef Marine Park

One of the seven natural wonders of the world and a UNESCO World Heritage site is the Great Barrier Reef. It is the largest coral reef system in the world, stretching over 2,300 kilometers (1,430 miles) along Queensland's coast. A haven for marine biodiversity, the Great Barrier Reef Marine Park is home to a variety of coral formations, colorful fish, turtles, dolphins, and even whales during their migratory season. You may fully immerse yourself in this underwater paradise while on snorkeling, scuba diving, and sailing trips, learning about the wonder and fragility of this extraordinary ecosystem.

Daintree Rainforest

The Daintree Rainforest, which is north of Cairns, is among the oldest and most diversified rainforests on the globe. The Wet Tropics of Queensland World Heritage Area includes an ancient tropical rainforest, which boasts a staggering variety of vegetation and fauna. On guided treks through the lush canopy, you can discover cascading waterfalls and go on a river boat to see crocodiles and other species. The Kuku Yalanji Aboriginal people share their traditional knowledge and spiritual ties to the land in the Daintree, which is also a significant cultural site.

Fraser Island

The biggest sand island in the world and a UNESCO World Heritage site is Fraser Island, often referred to as K'gari. This breathtaking natural wonder is home to pristine beaches, soaring sand dunes, verdant rainforests, and freshwater lakes with crystal pure water. Utilize a 4WD, hiking trails, or guided tours to explore the island's many ecosystems. Visit the renowned Lake McKenzie, known for its brilliant blue waters and pristine silica beaches, or explore Central Station's deep jungle depths. Visitors are in awe of Fraser Island's unspoiled beauty as a result of the diverse array of natural beauties it has to offer.

Whitsunday Islands

The Great Barrier Reef's central region is home to the 74 magnificent islands that make up the Whitsunday Islands archipelago. These idyllic islands include bright coral reefs, white, powdery beaches, and clear, turquoise water. Discover Whitehaven Beach, a landmark known for its stunning beauty and flawless silica sand. Visit the reef-fringed islands to snorkel or dive and see the abundant marine life there. With the chance to discover remote bays and anchorages in this tropical sanctuary, the Whitsunday Islands are a haven for sailors.

Carnarvon Gorge

Carnarvon Gorge, located in Outback Queensland, is a hidden gem that showcases the breathtaking grandeur of the area's ancient sandstone landscapes. The gorge has spectacular hiking routes that lead to Aboriginal rock art sites and breathtaking vistas, as well as high cliffs, picturesque waterholes, and breathtaking scenery. Set off on a trek into the gorge to experience the tranquil tranquility of this natural marvel while crossing chilly waterways and unusual vegetation. The Moss Garden, Amphitheatre, and the breathtaking Carnarvon Gorge itself, with its imposing sandstone cliffs, are among the attractions.

These Queensland natural wonders represent the state's unmatched beauty and highlight the variety of its landscapes, which range from coral reefs to rainforests, sandy beaches to steep gorges. Each presents a special chance to commune with nature, discover prehistoric ecosystems, and take in the astounding biodiversity that makes Queensland really exceptional. Queensland's natural wonders will enthrall and inspire you with the awe-inspiring power of nature, whether you're snorkeling with colorful marine life in the Great Barrier Reef, hiking through lush canopies of the Daintree Rainforest, or admiring the pristine beauty of Fraser Island and the Whitsunday Islands.

CHAPTER SIX:
Queensland's Coastal Cities and Towns

The dynamic and diverse coastal cities and towns of Queensland provide a unique blend of breathtaking natural beauty, cultural experiences, and a laid-back coastal lifestyle. Let's go further into six of Queensland's alluring seaside locations:

Brisbane

Brisbane, the capital of Queensland, is a thriving metropolis located along the Brisbane River. This thriving city offers the ideal blend of urban sophistication and natural beauty. Discover the South Bank Parklands, a riverbank sanctuary with flourishing markets, a man-made beach, and lush gardens. Explore the cultural district, which houses the Gallery of Modern Art, Queensland Art Gallery, and Queensland Museum. Take a stroll around

Fortitude Valley's energetic streets, which are popular for its live music venues, chic shops, and diverse food scene. Brisbane is a wonderful city to explore thanks to its lovely climate and welcoming atmosphere.

Gold Coast

Australia's playground, the Gold Coast is known for its magnificent beaches, exciting nightlife, and top-notch theme parks. The center of the activity is Surfers Paradise, which features a buzzing environment, towering residences, and a booming entertainment scene. Visit the well-known amusement parks, such as Dreamworld and Warner Bros. There are exhilarating rides, live entertainment, and interactions with marine life at Movie World and Sea World. Kilometers of stunning beachfront on the Gold Coast offer chances for swimming, surfing, and relaxing by the shore. With its jungles, waterfalls, and quaint mountain communities, the hinterland region offers an escape into nature.

Cairns

Cairns, which is located in Tropical North Queensland, serves as a gateway to the region's lush rainforests and the Great Barrier Reef. This bustling metropolis provides a relaxed tropical atmosphere and a variety of adventurous activities. Learn more about the Cairns Esplanade, a beachfront promenade packed with cafes, stores, and a swimming lagoon. Join a reef trip to snorkel or dive across the Great Barrier Reef's vibrant coral gardens. Visit the adjacent Daintree Rainforest, where you can go on a riverboat tour to see crocodiles or check out the breathtaking Mossman Gorge. Cairns is a center for Aboriginal cultural activities as well, providing opportunities to discover Indigenous history and customs.

Townsville

Townsville, a thriving city on Queensland's northeastern coast, is well-known for its breathtaking beaches, idyllic islands, and extensive cultural history. Discover The Strand, a waterfront promenade with a variety of restaurants and sweeping views of Magnetic Island. Learn about the Great Barrier Reef and its wonderful marine life at the well-known Reef HQ Aquarium, the biggest living coral reef aquarium in the world. Take a ferry to Magnetic Island, a naturalist's paradise with remote beaches, wildlife sightings, and hiking paths through national parks. Townsville is a well-liked vacation spot for both locals and tourists due to its warm climate and welcoming atmosphere.

Port Douglas

Port Douglas is a lovely coastal town that radiates carefree elegance. It is tucked between the Daintree Rainforest and the Great Barrier Reef. Take a stroll down Four Mile Beach, which is palm-lined and renowned for its spotless white sand and beautiful waters. Discover the upscale boutiques, galleries, and restaurants in the community. To explore the Great Barrier Reef's wonders, depart from Port Douglas on a reef cruise. Alternatively, take a picturesque drive to the adjacent Mossman Gorge for a thrilling jungle adventure. Port Douglas offers a serene and opulent vacation and acts as a gateway to the natural beauties of Tropical North Queensland.

Noosa

Noosa, a posh coastal town on Australia's Sunshine Coast, is well known for its immaculate beaches, breathtaking national parks, and lively food scene. Golden sand and calm surf make Noosa Main Beach ideal for swimming and sunbathing. Discover the Noosa National Park, where magnificent coastal pathways give breathtaking ocean views as they lead to secluded coves. Boutique stores, hip cafes, and top-notch restaurants dominate Hastings Street, which is a hive of activity. Water sports like kayaking, stand-up paddleboarding, and fishing are possible on the Noosa River. Beach lovers and outdoor enthusiasts flock to Noosa for its laid-back vibe and stunning surroundings.

These Queensland coastal cities and towns provide a variety of activities, including seaside leisure and exhilarating adventures, as well as urban discovery and cultural immersion. Queensland's coastal destinations promise a memorable and varied coastal experience for every traveler, whether you're exploring the cosmopolitan streets of Brisbane, taking in the vibrant energy of the Gold Coast, taking in the tropical wonders of Cairns and Townsville, indulging in luxury in Port Douglas, or embracing the laid-back charm of Noosa.

CHAPTER SEVEN:
Queensland's Adventure and Outdoor Activities

Queensland offers a wide range of thrilling outdoor activities, making it a haven for adventure seekers. Let's explore five exhilarating pursuits that highlight Queensland's spirit of exploration:

Scuba Diving and Snorkeling

Queensland is a well-known location for scuba diving and snorkeling since the Great Barrier Reef is right outside its door. Discover colorful marine life, explore brilliant coral gardens, and take in the beauty of the undersea world. The Whitsunday Islands, Cairns, Port Douglas, and the Outer Great Barrier Reef are popular spots for diving and snorkeling. Dive with tropical fish, rays, turtles, and a rainbow of other creatures, or snorkel in small lagoons filled with marine life. Divers of all levels will have a safe and memorable experience thanks to guided trips and experienced dive operators.

Surfing and Water Sports

The coastline of Queensland provides excellent chances for surfing and other water sports. The Gold Coast draws surfers from all over the world because of its top-notch surf breakers. Surfing novices can learn the sport from trained instructors, while advanced surfers can test their skills at world-famous spots like Burleigh Heads or Snapper Rocks. Another well-liked water sport is stand-up paddleboarding (SUP), which lets you explore serene coves and estuaries. For those who enjoy the water, there are a variety of water sports accessible, including jet skiing, kayaking, parasailing, and kiteboarding.

Hiking and Bushwalking

For nature lovers and outdoor enthusiasts, Queensland's various landscapes provide a variety of hiking and bushwalking trails. Glass House Mountains on the Sunshine Coast offer beautiful vistas from their summits, while Lamington National Park has a variety of routes that meander through historic rainforests and end at breathtaking waterfalls. Near Cairns, the Daintree Rainforest offers guided excursions that shed light on the distinctive flora and fauna of the area. Explore the numerous ecosystems on Fraser Island by hiking along the Great Walk, or travel to Outback Queensland's Carnarvon Gorge to see sandstone cliffs, old Indigenous rock art, and breathtaking views.

Skydiving and Bungee Jumping

In Queensland, exhilarating options for people wanting an adrenaline rush include skydiving and bungee jumping. Skydiving over gorgeous coastal settings like the Gold Coast or Mission Beach, where you may take in beautiful vistas before freefalling into the sky, will give you the ultimate rush of excitement. Bungee jumpers can attempt the jump from AJ Hackett's famous location in Cairns, where they will plummet into the lush rainforest with the breathtaking scenery as their backdrop. These extreme activities offer an exhilarating rush and a distinctive viewpoint of Queensland's breathtaking surroundings.

Wildlife Safaris and Whale Watching

The diverse fauna of Queensland presents chances for amazing encounters and wildlife excursions.

Visit the Steve Irwin Wildlife Reserve in the Sunshine Coast Hinterland to go on a safari and view kangaroos, koalas, and other well-known Australian creatures in their natural habitat. Visit Hervey Bay or the Great Barrier Reef during whale migration season for a marine wildlife adventure. Observe the majestic sight of humpback whales breaching and playing in the clear waters. A number of tour companies arrange whale-watching boats that allow visitors to get up close and personal with these spectacular animals.

Outdoor and adventure activities in Queensland appeal to both thrill-seekers and nature lovers. Whether you're scuba diving and snorkeling the Great Barrier Reef to discover its beauties, surfing the waves, taking on strenuous hikes in national parks, skydiving and bungee jumping to feel the excitement, or taking part in wildlife safaris and whale-watching cruises, you'll never run out of exciting things to do.

Queensland provides a wealth of chances to stretch your boundaries, engage with nature, and make unforgettable memories. Queensland is undoubtedly a sanctuary for outdoor enthusiasts thanks to its breathtaking scenery, diversified ecosystems, and profusion of marine life.

CHAPTER EIGHT:
Queensland's Aboriginal Heritage

Aboriginal culture, which dates back thousands of years, is active and rich throughout Queensland. Exploring the state's Aboriginal heritage offers a special chance to discover the customs, spirituality, and connection to the land that have influenced Queensland's Indigenous populations. Let's explore some of Queensland's Aboriginal heritage's diverse facets:

Cultural Centers and Tours

There are cultural centers all across Queensland that provide educational programs and immersive experiences to learn about Aboriginal culture. These facilities offer information about the history, culture, and traditions of the indigenous communities in the area. Indigenous guides who are informed about the culture can provide insight into the history of the Aboriginal people by highlighting important landmarks, telling stories, and engaging in customs. Examples include the Kuku Yalanji Cultural Habitat Tours in the Daintree Rainforest, the Quandamooka Cultural Centre in the Moreton Bay region, and the Tjapukai Aboriginal Cultural Park close to Cairns.

Rock Art Sites

Ancient rock art sites in Queensland offer a window into the religious and cultural customs of the Aboriginal people. These locations contain intricate and moving paintings and engravings that illustrate legends, religious beliefs, and a connection to the land. The rock art galleries in Carnarvon Gorge in Outback Queensland are well known for showcasing the Bidjara and Karingbal Aboriginal people's cultural history. An important cultural occasion that honors the local Aboriginal communities' storytelling and rock art traditions is the Laura Dance Festival in Cape York Peninsula.

Dreamtime Stories and Legends

The idea of the Dreamtime, sometimes referred to as the Dreaming or Creation Time, is fundamental to Aboriginal culture. Dreamtime tales and legends represent the spiritual values, origin stories, and ancestry of the Aboriginal people. These legends, which have been handed down through the generations, shed light on how people, the natural world, and the spiritual world interact. Visitors can learn more about the cultural significance and spiritual connection to the land through the sharing of these stories by Aboriginal guides and cultural centers.

Traditional Aboriginal Experiences

Queensland provides chances to participate in traditional Aboriginal activities that give direct exposure to cultural traditions and customs. Take part in activities like bush tucker (traditional cuisine) experiences, learning about old-fashioned hunting and gathering techniques, or taking part in a cleansing and protective smoking ceremony. Aboriginal tour guides impart their understanding of the environment, customary medical procedures, and the importance of music, dance, and language. Through these encounters, one might develop a deeper appreciation for Aboriginal culture and gain insight into the intergenerational bonds and resiliency of Queensland's Indigenous communities.

Aboriginal Art and Crafts

The distinctive and bright ways in which Aboriginal art expresses cultural heritage are well known. Talented Indigenous artists from Queensland express their stories, spiritual beliefs, and connection to the land via a variety of techniques, including painting, sculpture, weaving, and pottery. Queensland's cultural institutions and art galleries sell and exhibit Aboriginal art, giving the public a chance to appreciate and support these creators' efforts. To learn about traditional artistic methods and the cultural relevance of the artworks, visitors can also take part in seminars and demonstrations.

Visitors can better understand the complex cultural fabric that has defined Queensland by learning about its Aboriginal past. awareness of the enormous achievements and tenacity of Queensland's Aboriginal people requires an awareness of the linkages between the land, spirituality, and community. You can set out on a journey of cultural understanding, respect, and celebration of Queensland's diverse Aboriginal heritage through cultural centers, rock art locations, Dreamtime stories, traditional experiences, and the appreciation of Aboriginal art and crafts.

CHAPTER NINE:
Queensland's Cuisine and Dining Experiences

Queensland's cuisine is a reflection of the state's rich natural resources, numerous cultural influences, and love of locally obtained, fresh products. Queensland offers a culinary voyage that tempts the taste senses, from luscious seafood to distinctive bush tucker flavors and a blend of world cuisines. Let's examine the salient features of Queensland's cuisine and dining experiences in more detail:

Seafood and Fresh Produce

Queensland is a seafood lover's heaven with its long coastline and flourishing fishing industry. Queensland has a vast range of seafood pleasures, from the Great Barrier Reef's clear waters to its many rivers and estuaries. Enjoy freshly caught seafood such as barramundi, coral trout, mud crabs, and prawns, crabs, oysters, and a variety of fish. Moreton Bay, Hervey Bay, and the Sunshine Coast are well known for their mouthwatering seafood selections. Ample fresh fruits, vegetables, and tropical delicacies like mangoes, pineapples, and macadamia nuts are also produced by Queensland's lush lands, and these produce are used in the vibrant local cuisine.

Bush Tucker and Indigenous Cuisine

Indigenous people in Queensland have a rich culinary history that is firmly based in the land and its resources. Discover the distinct tastes of bush tucker, which includes native ingredients like wattleseed, quandong, emu, kangaroo, and bush tomatoes. Indigenous chefs and cultural institutions provide opportunities to sample traditional Indigenous cuisine, which combines modern flavors with age-old traditions and cooking methods. These meal occasions give you a better appreciation of how closely connected to the earth and rich in culture the Indigenous people are.

Fusion and International Cuisine

Queensland's culinary landscape embraces a blend of worldwide influences in addition to traditional tastes. The state's diversified character has led to a wide variety of international cuisines. You may find a fusion of cuisines from all around the world in everything from bustling food markets to acclaimed restaurants. Eat authentic Italian food at the thriving dining districts of the Gold Coast or indulge in Asian-inspired delicacies in Brisbane's Chinatown's bustling streets. Every palette may experience a gastronomic trip in Queensland thanks to the widespread celebration of international flavors from places like Greece, India, Japan, and the Middle East.

The allure of dining in Queensland extends beyond the plate due to the breathtaking surroundings. In waterfront restaurants with views of stunning beaches, savor freshly caught seafood, or enjoy your lunch amidst the thick rainforests of the Daintree. Additionally, lively food festivals and marketplaces all around the state offer chances to try regional specialties, talk to passionate food producers, and become immersed in the area's culinary culture.

Wineries and Wine Tasting

There are several beautiful winery districts in Queensland that create a diverse range of wines. Queensland's best wine region, the Granite Belt, is part of the Southern Downs and is known for its mild climate and award-winning wines. Discover wineries that produce crisp whites like Chardonnay and Verdelho as well as sophisticated reds like Shiraz and Cabernet Sauvignon. Enjoy wine tastings at cellar doors, where you may sample a variety of beverages and learn about the wine-making process from expert employees. Wine tasting in Queensland is a lovely and special experience because of the beautiful surroundings and elegant cellar doors.

Food Festivals and Markets

Food festivals and markets in Queensland honor the wealth of regional produce and highlight the area's culinary prowess. These gatherings create a lively and joyful environment for food enthusiasts, craftsmen, and producers. Renowned chefs, winemakers, and food fans travel from all over the country to attend the Noosa Food and Wine Festival, which is hosted in one of Queensland's most famous seaside towns. Brisbane's Regional Flavours festival honors the state's numerous food and drink options and includes cooking demonstrations, live music, and a variety of market booths. Farmers' markets in your area, including the well-known Eumundi Markets and the Davies Park Market in West End, give you the chance to sample and buy fresh produce, handmade goods, and mouth watering sweets straight from the manufacturers and growers.

These Queensland wineries, culinary festivals, and markets provide chances to sample fine wines, experience regional delicacies, and interact with enthusiastic producers. Queensland's wine and food experiences are a celebration of the region's gourmet offers and the enthusiasm of its producers, whether you're immersing yourself in the Granite Belt's vineyards, sampling the culinary pleasures at food festivals, or wandering through bustling markets.

Queensland's culinary environment is a combination of tastes, textures, and cultural influences, whether you're relishing the flavors of the sea, experiencing the distinctive tastes of bush tucker, or traveling the world through various cuisines. Enjoy the richness of Indigenous ingredients, the freshness of locally sourced products, and the innovation of fusion and international cuisine. The eating and dining experiences in Queensland provide a genuinely unforgettable culinary trip that highlights the state's rich culinary tradition and enthusiasm for food.

CHAPTER TEN:
Historical Sites and Landmarks in Queensland

Queensland has a long history, and there are many historical monuments and landmarks there that depict its past. The state offers a fascinating trip through its varied past, from colonial colonies to Indigenous historical sites. Let's examine the main characteristics of Queensland's historical sites and landmarks in more detail:

Historical Towns and Settlements

There are numerous towns and villages in Queensland that have contributed significantly to the state's history. Discover locations like Cooktown, where Captain James Cook first set foot on Australian soil in 1770, marking the beginning of recorded European contact with the region. The second-largest city in Queensland during the gold rush, Charters Towers, is home to exquisite heritage structures that reflect a bygone era. With more than 600 buildings on the National Register of Historic Places, the town of Ipswich has a rich architectural history that reflects its importance as an early colonial settlement.

Colonial Architecture

Colonial architecture is prominent in Queensland, a reflection of the state's early European colonization and the Victorian and Federation eras' influence. The Old Government House, Customs House, and the Treasury Building are just a few of Brisbane's outstanding colonial buildings. Cities in regional areas with spectacular heritage structures and opulent Victorian-era mansions include Maryborough and Toowoomba. These historical treasures offer a window into the past and are a testimony to the state's colonial past.

Heritage-listed Buildings

There are many heritage-listed structures in Queensland, which preserve and highlight the state's architectural and historical significance. In the center of the city, the recognizable Brisbane City Hall, with its recognizable clock tower, is a significant heritage landmark. While the Abbey Museum of Art and Archaeology in Caboolture displays a collection of antiquities and artifacts from ancient civilizations, the Wolston Farmhouse near Brisbane offers an insight into early farming life. Queensland's heritage-listed buildings, which range in size from opulent public structures to modest cottages, serve as a reminder of the state's rich architectural and historical past.

Museums and Historical Exhibits

Intense historical experiences are available at Queensland's historical sites and museums. Through its exhibits on dinosaurs, Indigenous civilizations, and early settlers, the Queensland Museum in Brisbane offers insights into the state's natural and cultural history. Townsville's Museum of Tropical Queensland highlights the region's maritime heritage, including the intriguing tale of the HMS Pandora and its connection to the illustrious Mutiny on the Bounty. The Cobb+Co Museum in Toowoomba honors the state's transportation history by showcasing a variety of horse-drawn carriages and pioneer-era items.

Indigenous Heritage Sites

Numerous major locations in Queensland allow visitors to learn more about the region's Indigenous heritage. Ancient rock art from the Cape York Peninsula's Quinkan Galleries offers a window into Indigenous cultural practices and traditions. Local Indigenous guides provide guided tours at the Ngadiku Dreamtime Walk in the Daintree Rainforest, sharing the legends, culture, and spirituality of the area. In Tjapukai, close to Cairns, the Aboriginal Cultural Park offers an immersive experience where guests may learn about Indigenous practices, art, and dance.

It is possible to gain a deeper understanding of Queensland's legacy, culture, and the various communities that have influenced the state by touring its historical sites and landmarks. You'll discover the layers of history that have molded Queensland into the dynamic state it is today, whether you're exploring the streets of historical towns, taking in the colonial architecture, visiting museums, or immersing yourself in Indigenous cultural sites.

CHAPTER ELEVEN:
Queensland's Festivals and Events

Festivals and events in Queensland serve as a platform for the state's thriving culture, creativity, and sense of community. Queensland has a wide variety of festivals and events that draw both locals and tourists, from the aesthetic extravaganza of the Brisbane Festival to the celebration of Indigenous art and culture at the Cairns Indigenous Art Fair. Here are some of Queensland's most notable festivals and events, in more detail:

Brisbane Festival

The Brisbane Festival is a yearly multi-arts event that turns the city into a hive of inspiration and excitement. The festival, which spans three weeks, offers a varied schedule of acts, including music, dance, theater, and visual arts. Highlights include the

Riverfire fireworks display, which illuminates the Brisbane River, and the Night Noodle Markets, where guests may savor delectable Asian cuisine. The Brisbane Festival brings together the community to celebrate the arts in the center of the city by attracting both local and foreign artists.

Cairns Indigenous Art Fair

The Cairns Indigenous Art Fair (CIAF) is a one-of-a-kind celebration of the diversity, richness, and artistic expression of Aboriginal and Torres Strait Islander people. The Indigenous Contemporary and Traditional Art Festival (CIAF), which takes place every year in Cairns, offers a venue for artists to display and market their creations. Visitors can take in lively seminars, fashion presentations, cultural acts, and exhibitions of art. The CIAF also provides the chance to interact with artists in person and discover their histories, customs, and artistic processes.

Gold Coast Commonwealth Games

Athletes from all around the Commonwealth came together for the Gold Coast Commonwealth Games, a significant international athletic event. The 2018 Games served as a showcase for the Gold Coast's breathtaking beaches, cutting-edge sporting venues, and energetic environment. The event featured a variety of sports, from swimming and cycling to gymnastics and athletics, creating exciting events and unforgettable experiences for both competitors and spectators.

Woodford Folk Festival

An iconic occasion is the Woodford Folk Festival, which takes place every year in Woodford,

Queensland. One of the biggest outdoor events in Australia, it draws musicians, artists, and tourists from all over the world. The festival features a varied program of visual arts seminars, music, dance, and drama. Participants can camp out under the stars, immerse themselves in a distinctive communal environment, and participate in discussions and debates about social and environmental issues. The Woodford Folk Festival is a highlight of Queensland's cultural calendar because of its reputation for being welcoming and family-friendly.

Port Douglas Carnivale

A thriving local event, Port Douglas Carnivale honors the area's natural beauty and tropical way of life. The festival features live music, street parades, art exhibits, wine and cuisine events, and family-friendly activities to highlight the finest of

Port Douglas. Visitors can take in the vibrant and energetic Carnivale Parade or indulge in the mouth watering flavors of the Longest Lunch, an outdoor eating experience showcasing regional fare. The Port Douglas Carnivale offers a vibrant and joyous ambiance that captures the character of the area.

Queensland's festivals and events showcase the state's rich cultural diversity, outstanding artistic talent, and sense of community. Queensland's festivals and events offer memorable experiences that highlight the best of the state's culture, creativity, and community, whether you're immersing yourself in the artistic wonders of the Brisbane Festival, celebrating Indigenous art and culture at the Cairns Indigenous Art Fair, taking in the sporting prowess of the Gold Coast Commonwealth Games, experiencing the creative energy of the Woodford Folk Festival, or

participating in the festivities of Port Douglas
Carnivale.

CHAPTER TWELVE:
Practical Information for Travelers

It's crucial to be aware of useful information that can improve your vacation and make your time in Queensland more enjoyable. Here are some important things for travelers to remember:

Transportation Options

The state of Queensland has a variety of transportation choices that make getting around easy and accessible. Public transportation systems, which include buses, trains, and ferries, offer dependable and reasonably priced ways to move around in big cities like Brisbane and Gold Coast. There are frequent bus services in regional areas that link towns and cities. For traveling to distant locations and exploring local areas, renting a car is a common option. Additionally, Queensland has a number of domestic airports that provide service to numerous locations within the state and provide connections to other Australian regions.

Money and Currency Exchange

Australia uses the Australian Dollar (AUD) as its official currency. For smaller transactions, it is essential to have some cash on hand, especially in rural locations. You can withdraw cash from ATMs using the most popular credit and debit cards, which are readily available. Although most hotels, restaurants, and retail establishments now take credit cards, it's still a good idea to have some cash on hand in case a particular establishment does not. Although banks may offer better rates, major airports and some metropolitan areas offer currency exchange services.

Language and Cultural Etiquette

The majority of people in Queensland speak English, which is the country's official language. It should be simple for English-speaking travelers to communicate. It's crucial to remember that certain populations, especially in isolated locations, also speak Indigenous languages. Australians tend to be amiable and informal when it comes to cultural etiquette. Respect for cultural diversity is highly regarded, thus it's crucial to be conscious and respectful of Indigenous traditions and practices when visiting Aboriginal communities or heritage sites. It's usual to greet individuals with a smile and a simple "hello" or "g'day."

It's also important to note that Queensland has a laid-back and informal way of life that emphasizes outdoor recreation and a love of the beach.

Comfortable, informal dress is typical, especially in coastal regions and small towns. However, smart-casual or professional dress may be appropriate in more formal situations like fine dining locations.

Other practical tips for travelers include:

- Climate: The climate in Queensland varies depending on the region. It's wise to research the local weather before traveling so you can pack appropriately. Queensland can have hot, muggy summers, and pleasant winters that can go colder in the south.

- Sun protection: Queensland has a lot of exposure to the sun. To shield yourself from the sun's UV rays, it's necessary to use sunscreen, a hat, sunglasses, and to seek shade during the hottest parts of the day.

- Health and Safety: Although Queensland has first-rate medical facilities; it's a good idea to obtain travel insurance to cover any unexpected medical costs. Additionally, it's crucial to take safety precautions when participating in outdoor sports and water-based excursions, especially in hot and humid weather.

- Time Zones: Queensland is in the UTC +10:00 time zone and follows Australian Eastern Standard Time (AEST). However, during the summer, some areas of Queensland, particularly those in the south, follow daylight saving time and switch to Australian Eastern Daylight Time (AEDT), which is UTC +11:00.

Safety Tips and Emergency Contacts

It's critical to prioritize your safety and be cognizant of potential threats when visiting Queensland. Observe the following safety advice:

- Be sure to familiarize yourself with local rules and ordinances to make sure you observe them while you are there.

- Take safety measures to guard your personal possessions, such as keeping an eye on them in crowded places and putting valuables in hotel safes.

- Be aware of any warning flags or signs indicating the presence of strong currents or harmful marine creatures when swimming at beaches or in natural waterways. Swim between the prescribed areas while adhering to lifeguard instructions.

- In tropical areas, keep an eye out for potentially dangerous species, such as snakes or stinging insects. It's best to stick to designated routes and ask local officials or tour guides for advice.

- Drink plenty of water and shield your skin from the heat by using a hat, sunscreen, and light-colored clothing. In order to prevent heat-related illnesses, it's vital to take precautions because Queensland's climate may be harsh, especially during the summer.

- Become familiar with the emergency phone numbers, such as 000 for non-mobile emergencies or 112 for mobile emergencies. You can reach the necessary emergency services, such as the police, fire, or ambulance, by dialing these numbers.

Health and Medical Services

The healthcare facilities and services in Queensland are of a very high caliber. It's crucial to have travel insurance that pays for any conceivable medical crises or out-of-pocket healthcare costs while you're away. Here are some important things to keep in mind when it comes to health and medical services in Queensland:

- Speak with a medical expert prior to your trip to confirm that you are up-to-date on both standard vaccinations and any particular immunizations advised for the area you want to visit.

- Queensland has a network of general practitioners (GPs), hospitals, and clinics that can offer medical treatment if you need it. You can go to a general practitioner or medical facility for treatment of minor diseases or injuries in non-emergency situations.

- To contact emergency services in the event of a medical emergency, dial 000. The operators will be able to direct you and send out the required medical aid.

- Pharmacies, also referred to as chemists in Australia, are easily accessible in the majority of towns and cities. They can offer guidance and over-the-counter treatments for mild illnesses.

- People who have pre-existing medical illnesses should make sure they have enough of the appropriate drugs and bring any necessary prescriptions or medical records.

It's usually a good idea to obtain travel insurance that includes medical emergencies because it can offer financial security and peace of mind in the event of unanticipated medical complications. Additionally, become familiar with the contact details for the consulate or embassy of your home country, as they may be able to help you in specific circumstances.

You may travel in Queensland safely and worry-free while knowing that you have access to high-quality healthcare facilities if you keep these practical issues in mind, are aware of safety precautions, are familiar with emergency contacts, and are prepared for any potential health concerns. Additionally, you may easily traverse Queensland, maximize your trip, and guarantee a memorable and pleasurable experience in this stunning Australian state.

CHAPTER THIRTEEN:
Shopping and Souvenirs in Queensland

Queensland provides visitors with a pleasant shopping experience, with options ranging from crowded malls to energetic marketplaces. Queensland has something to satisfy any shopper's taste, whether they are searching for distinctive souvenirs, Indigenous art and crafts, stylish swimwear, or local produce. Let's delve deeper into a few of the state's top shopping destinations:

Shopping Malls and Markets

Queensland is home to numerous shopping malls and centers, particularly in major cities like Brisbane, Gold Coast, and Cairns. These modern shopping centers offer a variety of retail establishments, including department stores, specialty shops, worldwide fashion brands, and entertainment venues. Brisbane's Queen Street Mall, the Gold Coast's Pacific Fair, and Cairns Central are a few well-known retail venues.

Visit one of the colorful markets dotted around Queensland for a distinctive shopping experience. A wide variety of goods are available in the markets, including fresh local fruit, handcrafted goods, jewelry, apparel, and much more. Eumundi marketplaces on the Sunshine Coast, Kuranda Markets close to Cairns, and South Bank Lifestyle Market in Brisbane are a few famous marketplaces. These markets offer the chance to buy unique items, sample regional specialties, and support local craftspeople.

Indigenous Art and Crafts

Shopping for Indigenous art and crafts is a meaningful way to connect with this history. Queensland is rich in Indigenous culture. Indigenous art is well known for its vivid hues, elaborate patterns, and storytelling. In Queensland, paintings, sculptures, didgeridoos, and boomerangs are just a few of the many Indigenous works of art on display in art galleries and specialty shops. These works frequently feature natural landscapes, ancestral spirits, and dream-like narratives. Purchasing Indigenous art supports Indigenous artists and their communities in addition to allowing you to acquire a one-of-a-kind object of cultural importance.

Fashion and Swimwear

Queensland is a fashion and swimwear hotspot due to its coastal lifestyle and mild environment. Cities like Brisbane, Gold Coast, and Noosa provide a wide variety of apparel options, from trendy boutiques to designer labels. Queensland's fashion scene has you covered whether you're seeking for beachwear, resort wear, or chic metropolitan clothes. There are many places to buy swimwear, and they come in many various shapes, sizes, and styles to fit different tastes and body types. Some coastal communities even have in-house swimwear manufacturers that offer distinctive and stylish options.

Local Produce and Souvenirs

You can buy a wide variety of tasty mementos to take home in Queensland, which is famed for its fresh and delicious local produce. There is something for every palate, from macadamia nuts and locally made chocolates to tropical fruits like mangoes and pineapples. Take advantage of the chance to visit farmers' markets and roadside stands where you can buy fresh produce, specialty foods, and delectable sweets.

In terms of mementos, Queensland provides a variety of choices. Look for souvenirs that embody the spirit of the area, such as T-shirts, magnets, postcards, and keychains with pictures of famous buildings or natural wonders. Additionally, locally produced handcrafted things like timber goods or pottery can make for interesting souvenirs.

Aboriginal Artifacts and Jewelry

Queensland is home to a wealth of jewelry and relics from the Aboriginal people. These products are a reflection of the Indigenous people's rich cultural heritage and long-standing customs. Boomerangs, didgeridoos, traditional tools, and ceremonial items are examples of Aboriginal artifacts. Native

American jewelry frequently combines organic materials like shells, beads, and bush seeds to produce gorgeous designs that convey a connection to the earth and ancient spirits. Look for reputable galleries and stores specializing in Indigenous art and artifacts to ensure the authenticity and ethical sourcing of these cultural treasures.

It's crucial to respect the cultural value of Aboriginal jewelry and artifacts while purchasing either of these products. For genuine and ethically sourced items, look for galleries or shops that collaborate with Indigenous artists and communities. Supporting indigenous artists helps to maintain their cultural heritage, as well as their communities' well-being and the practice of fair trade.

In summary, shopping in Queensland is a pleasure that provides a wide variety of possibilities. There are several options for apparel, regional produce, souvenirs, and Indigenous art and crafts available everywhere from contemporary retail complexes to bustling marketplaces. Get to know the people, buy from local makers, and bring home one-of-a-kind items that showcase Queensland's beauty and history.

CHAPTER FOURTEEN:
Nightlife and Entertainment in Queensland

The nightlife culture in Queensland is active and diversified, catering to a variety of tastes and inclinations. Queensland boasts a variety of options to keep you occupied late into the night, whether you're looking for hopping pubs and clubs, live music venues, cultural events, casino gambling, or outdoor film experiences. Let's delve deeper into these facets of Queensland's nightlife and entertainment:

Bars and Clubs

Major cities in Queensland, like Brisbane, Gold Coast, and Cairns, have a wide variety of bars and clubs that offer different types of music and atmospheres. There is something for everyone, from classy rooftop pubs with panoramic views to pulsating dance clubs with well-known DJs. Fortitude Valley in Brisbane is especially well-known for its vibrant bar culture, which features a variety of chic cocktail bars, live music venues, and late-night clubs. With its thriving bars and beachfront clubs, Surfers Paradise on the Gold Coast is a well-known destination for nightlife.

Live Music Venues

The live music scene in Queensland is growing and features both national and international artists from a variety of genres. There are numerous pubs, clubs, and live music venues that regularly host events and shows, giving people the chance to see up-and-coming performers or appreciate well-known bands. Particularly Brisbane's Fortitude Valley is well known for its live music establishments, such as The Triffid and The Zoo.

Both the QPAC Concert Hall in South Bank and the Tivoli in Fortitude Valley are larger venues that host well-known local, national, and worldwide performers.

Cultural Performances and Shows

Attend live performances and shows to really experience Queensland's rich cultural scene. The Queensland Performing Arts Centre (QPAC) in Brisbane presents a varied calendar of opera, musical, theater, and dance productions all year round. Another cultural hotspot in Brisbane is The Powerhouse, which presents a variety of shows, exhibits, and festivals. Regional hubs with theaters and cultural venues that present both local and traveling shows include Cairns, Townsville, and the Sunshine Coast.

Casino and Gaming

There are a number of top-notch casinos in Queensland for individuals looking for an exciting and opulent evening. Table games, video poker machines, and other forms of gaming are available at The Treasury Casino in Brisbane, The Star on the Gold Coast, and The Ville Resort-Casino in Townsville. These locations also have a variety of pubs, eateries, and entertainment options, offering a full range of entertainment options.

Outdoor Cinemas and Festivals

Enjoy the lovely weather in Queensland and the allure of outdoor movie experiences. You may unwind beneath the stars while watching the newest blockbusters or timeless movies thanks to the numerous cities and towns that hold outdoor cinema screenings in parks, gardens, and coastal areas. The Moonlight Cinema in Brisbane, Flickerfest in Port Douglas, and the Openair Cinemas on the Gold Coast are a few examples of well-liked outdoor film events.

Queensland is also well known for its celebrations of music, the arts, gastronomy, and culture. There is always something going on in Queensland to suit a variety of interests and tastes, from the Brisbane Festival, which features a varied range of acts and entertainment, to rural events like the Cairns Festival and the Blues on Broadbeach Music Festival.

In conclusion, Queensland has a thriving, varied, and catered nightlife and entertainment sector. You'll find lots of options to keep you engaged, whether you're looking for hopping bars and clubs, live music performances, cultural shows, casino gambling, or outdoor film experiences. Discover Queensland's exciting nightlife and entertainment options, take advantage of the dynamic atmosphere, and make lifelong experiences.

CHAPTER FIFTEEN:
Road Trips and Scenic Drives in Queensland

Queensland offers a wide variety of beautiful drives that highlight the state's natural beauty, well-known landmarks, and undiscovered jewels, making it a heaven for road trip aficionados. Queensland's picturesque drives and road trips have it all, whether you're looking for ocean views, untamed outback scenery, lush rainforests, or flowing waterfalls. Here are five famous roads that will take you on travels you won't soon forget:

Great Barrier Reef Drive

From Cairns to Cape Tribulation, there is a spectacular coastline path known as the Great Barrier Reef Drive. This breathtaking trip follows the coastline and offers breathtaking views of the

Coral Sea, immaculate beaches, and verdant jungles. You'll pass by charming coastal communities like Port Douglas and Mossman along the route, where you can explore the reef, engage in water sports, or take a cruise to see crocodiles in the Daintree River. The journey ends in Cape Tribulation, a particularly distinctive and alluring location where the rainforest meets the reef.

Pacific Coast Way

The Pacific Coast Way is a well-liked road travel route that runs over 1,700 kilometers from the Gold Coast to Cairns. You pass through a variety of scenery on this route, including glistening beaches, quaint coastal villages, national parks, and well-known sights. Along the journey, you may take in the grandeur of the Whitsunday Islands, discover the bustling city of Brisbane, unwind on the picturesque Sunshine Coast beaches, and pay a visit to the Australia Zoo. The Pacific Coast Way is a must-do road trip in Queensland because it combines natural marvels, adventurous pursuits, and cultural experiences.

Savannah Way

The 3,700-kilometer-long Savannah Way offers an incredible cross-country drive from Cairns to Broome for anyone looking for an outback experience. This journey takes you through the lonely and rocky outback of Queensland, where you may see wide-open plains, historic gorges, magnificent waterfalls, and rare fauna. You'll pass by well-known locations along the road, including Undara Volcanic National Park, Boodjamulla (Lawn Hill) National Park, and the untamed Gulf Savannah region. The Savannah Way offers visitors a complete immersion in the unspoiled splendor of the Australian outback.

Outback Adventure Drive

A mesmerizing drive through Outback Queensland's highlights is The Outback Adventure Drive. You pass through well-known outback communities along this route, like Longreach, Winton, and Mount Isa, where you can learn about Australia's early settlers, visit museums, and even see dinosaur fossils. Admire the breathtaking scenery of the enormous cattle stations, red dirt plains, and dramatic gorges like the Carnarvon Gorge and Boodjamulla National Park. You may fully experience Outback Queensland's rich culture and untamed scenery by taking the Outback Adventure Drive.

Waterfall Way

The Waterfall Way is a charming road that travels from Coffs Harbour to Armidale while winding through the breathtaking New England Tablelands. Despite being officially in New South Wales, this route is frequently included in itineraries for Queensland because of the state's accessibility and proximity to it. You pass through lush rainforests, gushing waterfalls, and quaint mountain communities on the route. Dangar Falls, Ebor Falls, the lovely hamlet of Bellingen, and Dorrigo National Park are a few of the highlights along the route. The Waterfall Way is a tranquil and picturesque route that highlights the area's unspoiled splendor.

These road trips and scenic drives offer travelers the opportunity to experience Queensland's diverse landscapes, from the iconic Great Barrier Reef to the rugged outback and everything in between. Whether you're seeking coastal beauty, rainforest immersion, outback adventure, or breathtaking waterfalls, these road trips cater to various interests and provide unforgettable experiences.

It's crucial to prepare ahead of time for these road excursions and to have a sturdy car that is appropriate for the terrain. When traveling through distant places, it is especially important to evaluate the distance, the availability of gasoline, and the state of the roads. Pack additional necessities like a first aid kit, water, food, and maps or other navigational aids to help you find your way.

Take the time to investigate and adjust your itinerary as necessary because every road trip offers distinctive sights and experiences. Think about the attractions, lodging choices, and any fees or permissions required. It's also important to keep in mind that various seasons, such as wet weather or closures due to bushfires, may necessitate taking extra measures along specific routes. Keep abreast of local news and, before leaving, check for any advisories.

Embrace the freedom and adventure that come with exploring these road excursions, immerse yourself in the grandeur of Queensland's landscapes, make pit stops at picturesque lookouts, and take leisurely strolls to find hidden jewels. As you travel across Queensland's intriguing areas, capture the breathtaking sights, get in touch with nature, and make lifelong memories.

In conclusion, Queensland's scenic drives and road trips provide a wide range of chances to learn about the state's natural treasures, cultural history, and distinctive landscapes. Whether you decide to travel the Great Barrier Reef Drive's coastal splendor, the Savannah Way's desert adventure, or the Waterfall Way's flowing beauty, each journey will give you a profound appreciation for Queensland's diverse and breathtaking sites. So fasten your seatbelt, hit the road, and go on a memorable journey across Queensland's road trip attractions.

CHAPTER SIXTEEN:
Conclusion and Farewell to Queensland

It's time to consider the amazing encounters, natural wonders, cultural encounters, and unique events that have formed your trip through the dynamic and diverse state of Queensland as it comes to an end. Queensland has made an enduring impression on your heart and mind, from the breathtaking coastline to the beautiful rainforests, from the vibrant cities to the peaceful outback.

We have examined the fundamental and comprehensive guide to Queensland's accommodations, dining options, shopping advice, insider secrets, top attractions, history, and culture throughout this book. We have explored the areas, learning about undiscovered treasures, natural wonders, coastal cities and towns, adventure activities, Aboriginal history, gastronomic delights, historical places, festivals, useful information, and more.

Queensland has made a point of showcasing its distinct beauty and allure, asking you to take in its stunning scenery, come face to face with its varied animals, learn about its fascinating history, and interact with its thriving communities. Queensland definitely made a lasting impact, whether you visited the energetic streets of Brisbane, surfed the waves of the Gold Coast, waded through the age-old Daintree Rainforest, or awed at the wonders of the Great Barrier Reef.

Keep in mind to bring your vacation memories from Queensland with you as you say goodbye to this lovely state. Keep in mind the breathtaking sunsets, thrilling experiences, friendly encounters with locals, and sense of amazement that Queensland has given you. Keep the photos, journals, and trinkets as a reminder of this amazing experience.

But this is not where Queensland's tale ends. It keeps changing, providing fresh chances for discovery as well as experiences and locations. The state continues to be an alluring location for tourists seeking adventure, relaxation, and cultural immersion even as it thrives and accepts change.

So, as you bid Queensland farewell, think back on the friendliness of its residents, the splendor of its landscapes, and the spirit of adventure that followed you on your journey. Keep Queensland's spirit close to your heart and let it guide your future journeys and explorations.

Queensland, I'll miss you until we next cross paths. Your warmth, variety, and beauty will live on in our hearts forever, beckoning us to return and discover more of your delights. I'm grateful for the experiences, memories, and enduring impressions. Queensland, you have been a genuinely remarkable place to visit.

Happy travels and may your life's journey be full with joyous exploration, discovery, and new experiences.

CHAPTER SEVENTEEN:
Appendix

You can find a variety of helpful tools and information in this appendix to make the most of your visit to Queensland; currency conversion table and a complete packing list.

Currency Conversion Chart

Please note that currency exchange rates fluctuate, and it's always advisable to check the most recent rates before your trip. The rates provided below are for reference purposes only.

1 AUD (Australian Dollar) equals:

- 0.72 USD (United States Dollar)

- 0.61 EUR (Euro)

- 0.53 GBP (British Pound)

- 1.04 CAD (Canadian Dollar)

- 80.15 JPY (Japanese Yen)

- 57.97 INR (Indian Rupee)

- 1.14 NZD (New Zealand Dollar)

- 0.77 CHF (Swiss Franc)

- 4.29 CNY (Chinese Yuan Renminbi)

- 0.87 SGD (Singapore Dollar)

Please note that exchange rates may vary and it's always a good idea to check with a reliable currency exchange service or financial institution for the most accurate and up-to-date rates before making any conversions.

Packing List for Queensland

Packing for your Queensland vacation requires careful consideration of the state's climate, landscapes, and activities. Here's a comprehensive packing list to ensure you have everything you need:

Clothing:

- Lightweight and breathable clothing for warm weather
- Swimwear for beach and water activities
- Hat and sunglasses for sun protection
- Light jacket or sweater for cooler evenings
- Comfortable walking shoes or hiking boots
- Flip flops or sandals
- Raincoat or umbrella (especially during the wet season)
- Active wear for adventure activities

Essentials:

- Valid passport and travel documents
- Travel adapters for electrical outlets
- Sunscreen with high SPF
- Insect repellent
- Personal medications and a small first aid kit
- Reusable water bottle

- Day backpack for day trips and hikes
- Waterproof bags for protecting electronic devices and documents

Electronics:
- Mobile phone and charger
- Camera or GoPro for capturing memories
- Power bank for charging devices on the go
- Portable Bluetooth speaker (optional)

Other Items:
- Travel guidebook and maps
- Snorkeling gear (if desired)
- Beach towel or sarong
- Travel pillow and blanket for long journeys
- Travel-sized toiletries
- Travel insurance documents
- Cash and/or credit cards

- Any specific items related to your interests or activities (e.g., binoculars for birdwatching, yoga mat for outdoor practice)

Remember to pack light and efficiently, considering the duration of your trip and the availability of laundry facilities at your accommodation. Be mindful of any specific requirements or restrictions for certain activities or attractions you plan to visit.

As you pack, also keep in mind the principles of sustainable travel, such as using eco-friendly toiletries, reducing single-use plastic items, and respecting the environment and local communities.

With this packing list, you'll be well-prepared for your Queensland adventure, ensuring a comfortable and enjoyable experience throughout your journey.

Safe travels and have a wonderful time exploring Queensland!

MAP OF QUEENSLAND

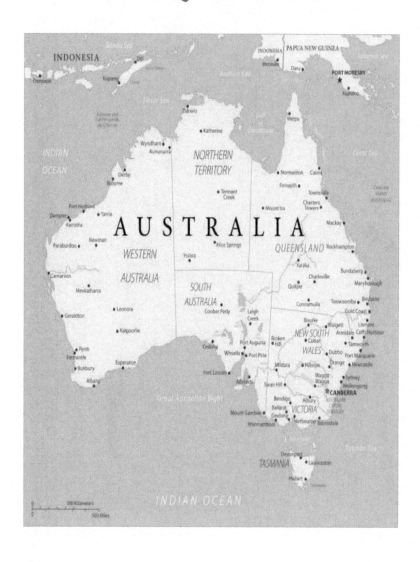

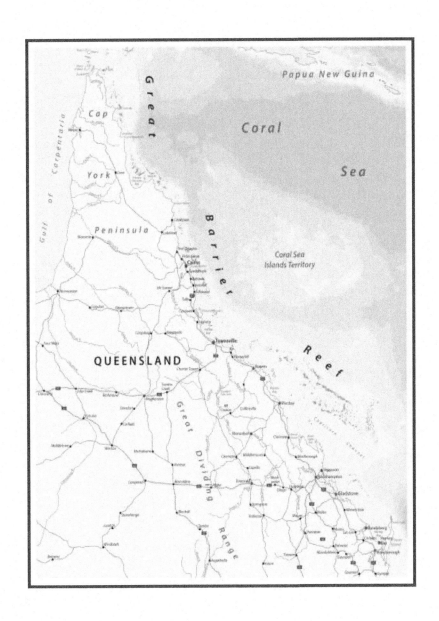

Printed in Great Britain
by Amazon